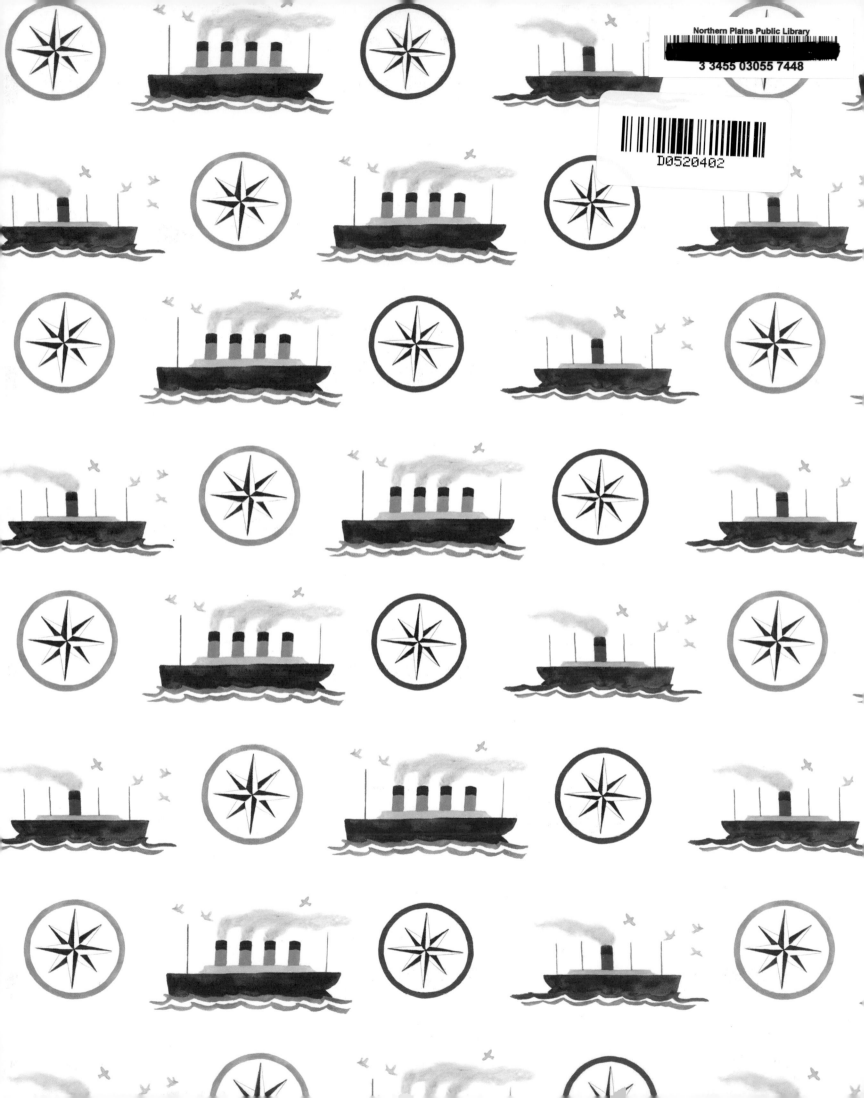

RESCUING
TITANIC

Flora Delargy

WIDE EYED EDITIONS

CONTENTS

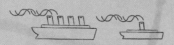

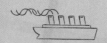

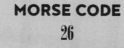

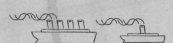

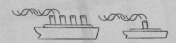

KEY CREW AND PASSENGERS

CARPATHIA

Captain Arthur
Rostron

Horace Dean,
First Officer

James Bisset,
Second Officer

Evan Hughes,
Chief Steward

Julia Czervenka,
Stewardess

Harold Cottam,
Wireless Operator

Percy Barnett,
Assistant Purser

Mary Hague,
Stewardess

Dr Frank McGee
Medic

Hettie Smith,
Stewardess

A.B. Johnston,
Chief Engineer

Amy Quayle,
Stewardess

Ernest Brown,
Purser

Bernice (Bernie) Palmer

Theresa Palmer

Louis Ogden

Augusta Ogden

Katherine Hurd

Carlos Hurd

Emma Lampert Cooper

Colin Campbell Cooper

TITANIC

Captain Edward Smith

Joseph Boxhall, 4th Officer

Harold Bride, Wireless Operator

Jack Phillips, Wireless Operator

Charles Lightoller, 2nd Officer

William Murdoch, 1st Officer

Mrs Luise Kink

Miss Luise Kink

Margaret (Molly) Brown

Olive Earnshaw

Margaret Hayes

Lady (Pomeranian)

Hudson River Harbor, New York, USA

The year was 1912 and it was the golden age of steam travel. In one of the world's busiest ports, great liners like floating hotels were docked, each hoping to outpace the other across the Atlantic.

Before steamships, ocean travel had been fraught with danger and journeys were long and tiresome.

By the end of the 1800s, powerful steamships were racing across the Atlantic in under eight days. With bigger and faster vessels, many more people were able to leave Europe in search of a new life in the USA. The more glamorous ships attracted a new type of wealthy traveler. It was an exciting time to travel. The docksides were buzzing on New York's Hudson River as families came to meet and see loved ones off on their extraordinary journeys.

RMS TITANIC

April 10, 1912
Southampton, UK

The grandest ship ever to take to the ocean, the RMS Titanic departed from Southampton bound for New York. She was the pride of the transatlantic White Star Line. She was nearly 900 ft long from bow to stern, 100 ft high from keel to bridge, and measured over 46,000 gross tons.

Built in Belfast, Northern Ireland, she was fitted with the most luxurious cabins, dining saloons, and cafés of the day.

Well-wishers and family waved from the dockside as the Titanic slipped her moorings and steamed out majestically. Meanwhile, the 900-strong crew busied themselves for the historic voyage to New York.

RMS CARPATHIA

April 11, 1912

Hudson River Harbor, New York, USA

As the world cheered the departure of the Titanic, a more modest and unspectacular ship called the RMS Carpathia prepared for her own voyage. She had been completed just nine years earlier in Tyneside, northern England, for the Cunard shipping line. The Carpathia had been designed to carry both cargo and passengers, most of whom were in second and third class accommodation.

The Carpathia's captain was Arthur Rostron. Born in 1869 near Bolton, Rostron started his life as a mariner at the age of 15 when he joined the training ship HMS Conway. Once at sea, he gathered experience and qualifications enabling him to work his way up the ranks. By 1907 he was given command of the cargo ship Brescia. Five years later he was delighted to be promoted to Captain of the Carpathia.

While the Titanic and her 1,300 passengers set sail westwards across the North Atlantic to New York, the Carpathia was quietly preparing to depart. She was to head east from Pier 54 on the Hudson River bound for Genoa, Naples, Trieste, and Fiume.

THE CARPATHIA CREW

The Carpathia had a crew of 300, each one of them with their own special responsibilities. As with other similar ships, there were three departments: deck crew, engine crew and victualling crew. Each department had a clear chain of command.

VICTUALLING CREW

The crew in this department was in charge of food, drink, and accommodation as well as on board security.

ENGINE CREW

The duties of the Engine crew involved ensuring the ship's engines and electrical power continued to run smoothly throughout the journey.

DECK CREW

This department was responsible for all nautical matters such as navigation and managing deck equipment.

In the days before departure, the Carpathia was loaded with supplies for the journey and cargo for transportation to Europe. The ship had three large refrigerated holds for transporting food, especially meat. On the Mediterranean routes, ships would often carry wheat, cotton, tobacco, and even metals and lumber. Everything was loaded with the help of the ship's 14 steam winches and 18 derricks.

PASSENGERS

The Carpathia's passengers came from all walks of life. Most were American tourists or Europeans who lived in the USA, traveling home to visit family. There were 122 passengers in first class, 41 in second class, and 571 in third class.

Louis and Augusta Ogden knew Captain Rostron from previous voyages. This journey was the first leg of a round-the-world tour.

Traveling with her mother, 18 year old Bernice Palmer was excited to document her trip to the Mediterranean with her new Kodak Box Brownie camera.

Traveling second class on the Carpathia, Journalist Carlos Hurd and his wife, Katherine were looking forward to their holiday in Europe.

Colin Campbell Cooper, a well-known artist, was traveling with his wife, Emma.

THE ROUTE

On the bridge, Rostron consulted his navigational charts prior to casting off.
The Carpathia was set on a route to the Mediterranean. The first stop was 4,000 miles
away in Gibraltar, a journey that would take 11 days.

EASTBOUND

40° 35° 30° 25° 20° 15° 10°

ATLANTIC OCEAN

IRELAND

30°

NEW YORK — QUEENSTOWN ROUTE

45°

45°

PORTUGAL

40°

AZORES

35°

40° 35° 30° 25° 20° 15° 10° 5°

The Carpathia would pass the Azores and through the Strait of Gibraltar, a narrow stretch of water connecting the Atlantic to the Mediterranean Sea. From there, she would call at ports such as Messina, Trieste, and Fiume.

NAVIGATION

Captain Rostron and his crew used a number of key tools to navigate long stretches of open ocean.

SEXTANT

For a very long time mariners had looked up to the sky to help work out their location at sea. Their preferred reference point was the sun. In time increasingly sophisticated instruments were invented to measure the angle between the horizon and the sun or stars.

The invention of the sextant was a major advancement. It meant sailors could accurately establish the latitude of the ship, that is how far north or south it was from the Equator.

CHARTS

Charts are maps of the sea. While the first world map was created around 2,600 years ago, the earliest nautical charts weren't made until the end of the 13th century. Initially, charts ignored the curvature of the Earth but by the 16th century, they took that into account.

Chronometers and sextants may tell sailors exactly how far they are from a particular location, but a chart makes that information visual! Charts not only depict shorelines in detail, they provide information about depth of water and hazards as the vessel draws closer to land.

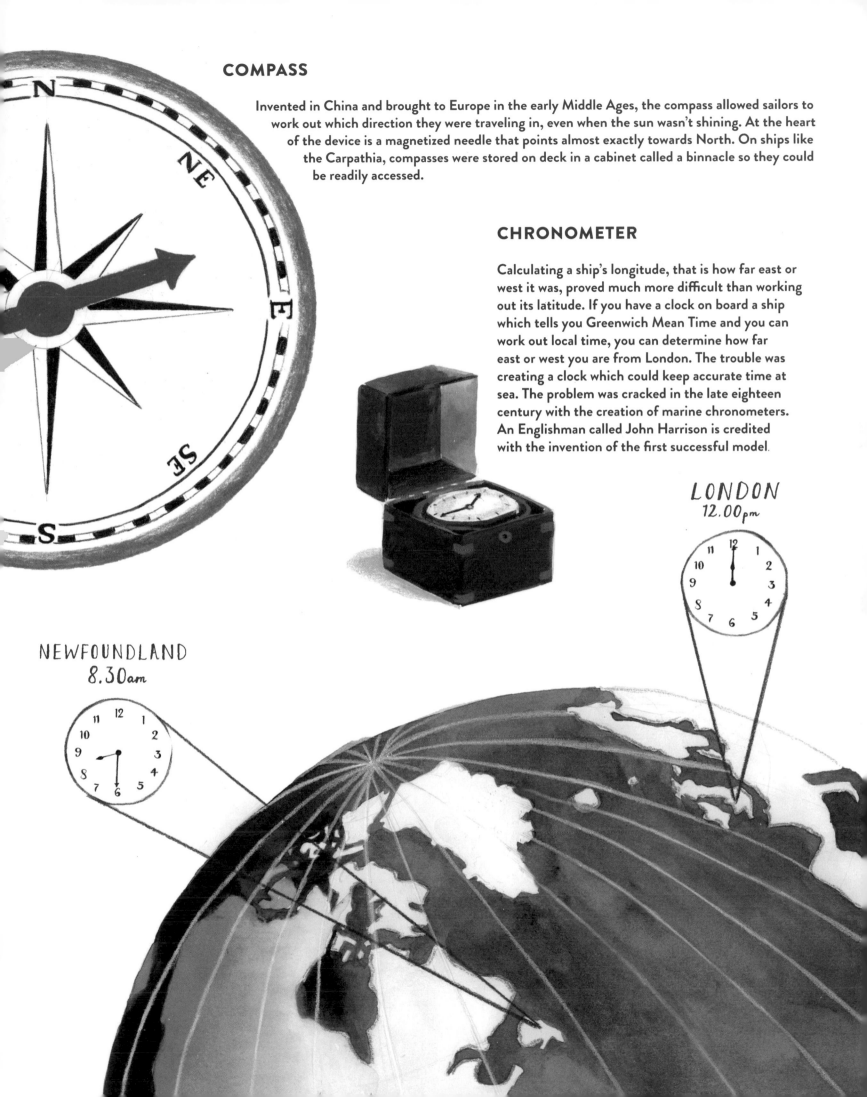

COMPASS

Invented in China and brought to Europe in the early Middle Ages, the compass allowed sailors to work out which direction they were traveling in, even when the sun wasn't shining. At the heart of the device is a magnetized needle that points almost exactly towards North. On ships like the Carpathia, compasses were stored on deck in a cabinet called a binnacle so they could be readily accessed.

CHRONOMETER

Calculating a ship's longitude, that is how far east or west it was, proved much more difficult than working out its latitude. If you have a clock on board a ship which tells you Greenwich Mean Time and you can work out local time, you can determine how far east or west you are from London. The trouble was creating a clock which could keep accurate time at sea. The problem was cracked in the late eighteen century with the creation of marine chronometers. An Englishman called John Harrison is credited with the invention of the first successful model.

LONDON
12.00pm

NEWFOUNDLAND
8.30am

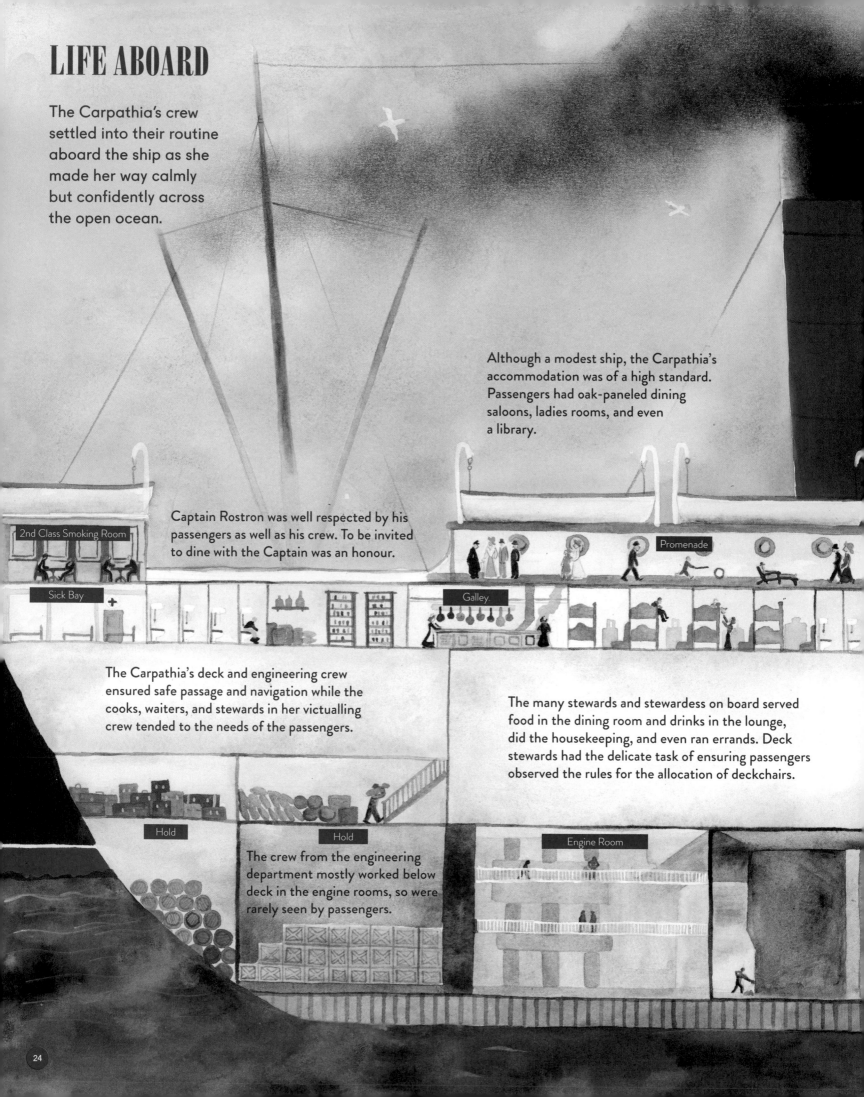

LIFE ABOARD

The Carpathia's crew settled into their routine aboard the ship as she made her way calmly but confidently across the open ocean.

Although a modest ship, the Carpathia's accommodation was of a high standard. Passengers had oak-paneled dining saloons, ladies rooms, and even a library.

Captain Rostron was well respected by his passengers as well as his crew. To be invited to dine with the Captain was an honour.

2nd Class Smoking Room

Promenade

Sick Bay

Galley.

The Carpathia's deck and engineering crew ensured safe passage and navigation while the cooks, waiters, and stewards in her victualling crew tended to the needs of the passengers.

The many stewards and stewardess on board served food in the dining room and drinks in the lounge, did the housekeeping, and even ran errands. Deck stewards had the delicate task of ensuring passengers observed the rules for the allocation of deckchairs.

Hold

Hold

Engine Room

The crew from the engineering department mostly worked below deck in the engine rooms, so were rarely seen by passengers.

Once a day, Captain Rostron and his officers would use their sextants to take sun sightings in order to discover the ship's position along its route. On ocean liners like the Carpathia the findings were of great interest to passengers, especially those who had taken a bet in the ship's sweepstake on how far the vessel had traveled each day.

Bridge

Captain and Officers' Quarters

Library

Barber Shop

2nd Class Cabins

1st Class Dining Room

3rd Class Dining Room

In addition to their shared dormitories or cabins, passengers in third class had access to their own public rooms and saloons.

3rd Class Cabins

Refrigerated Hold

Boilers

Coal Hold

Trimmers shoveled coal from the bunkers and gave it to the stokers who loaded it into seven boilers. The boilers created the steam to drive the engines. The power produced turned the Carpathia's two large propellers, enabling her to reach a comfortable speed of 14 knots.

MORSE CODE

In days gone by, when a ship was out on the high seas, it would be entirely out of communication with the world. The Italian inventor Guglielmo Marconi helped to change all that. By the end of the 19th century he had helped develop long distance wireless radio communication.

Liners were fitted with special radio equipment and trained operators used them to send and receive messages. These messages allowed ships to call for help via Morse code, an international system of dots, dashes, and spaces which represented numbers and letters of the alphabet.

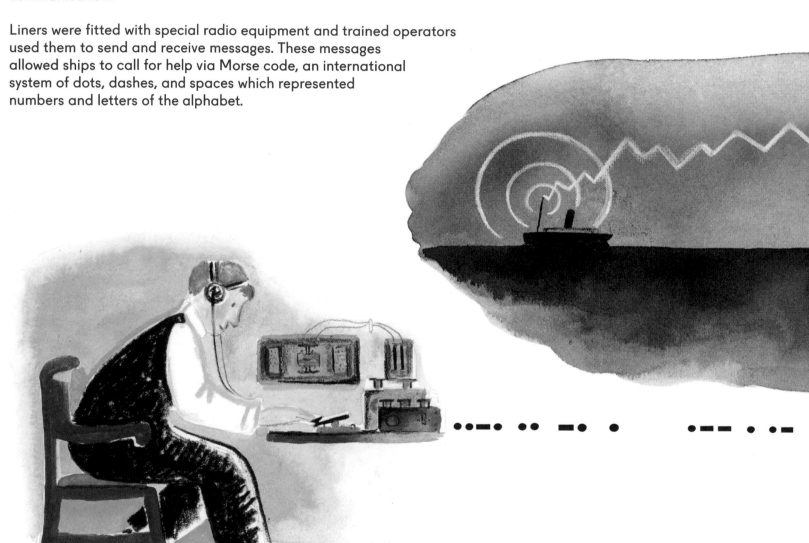

The radio operator on board the Carpathia was 21-year-old Harold Cottam, who had trained specially at the Marconi School in Liverpool. He spent up to 17 hours a day at the instrument table tapping out messages and listening to incoming traffic.

The messages were received by the Marconi antenna on top of one of the ship's four masts, and then were transmitted to the listening equipment. The Carpathia could send messages up to 200 miles away. The Titanic's Morse code transmissions were very advanced and they sounded almost musical.

International Morse Code Alphabet

A	•—		N	—•
B	—•••		O	———
C	—•—•		P	•——•
D	—••		Q	——•—
E	•		R	•—•
F	••—•		S	•••
G	——•		T	—
H	••••		U	••—
I	••		V	•••—
J	•———		W	•——
K	—•—		X	—••—
L	•—••		Y	—•——
M	——		Z	——••

On Sunday, April 14, Cottam noted some wireless reports of ice on sea routes further north. He left the Marconi Wireless Room, to deliver the communications to the Bridge where Second Officer James Bisset was on duty. He then returned to his post to resume his duties.

NIGHT FALLS ON  THE CARPATHIA

11pm Sunday, April 14

Captain Rostron was feeling very pleased with the Carpathia's steady progress. By now most of the passengers had retired to their cabins and dormitories and were settling down to bed. The stewards and stewardesses had turned off the lights in the library and dining saloons. Soon, they would help usher the last passengers to their cabins. Shortly, the Captain would retire to his own quarters. On this beautiful and cold, clear night, the deck crew on the late shift could see practically every star in the sky.

All was calm and in its place as the ship made its way through the dark water.

NIGHT FALLS ON  THE TITANIC

Not long after, on the Titanic, the still night was broken. Lookouts in the crow's nest had spotted an iceberg. They raised the alarm and the First Officer Murdoch issued orders for the ship to veer left and the engines to be thrust into reverse. It wasn't enough, and the largest ocean liner in the world struck the iceberg on her starboard side. Water began to flood in through several tears in her hull.

The Titanic's Captain Smith was alerted by the commotion and almost immediately arrived on the bridge. He instructed Fourth Officer Boxhall to commission a thorough inspection of the ship.

In the first ten minutes, five forward compartments had flooded. This was one too many to allow her to stay afloat. After assessing the damage, the ship's Belfast designer, Thomas Andrews told Captain Smith the ship would sink within 90 minutes. All of her 2,220 passengers and crew were now in great danger.

HARD TO STARBOARD!

THE TITANIC CALLS FOR HELP

Boxhall went to the chart room to calculate the ship's position. He determined it to be 41°46' North, 50°14' West. Captain Smith told him to pass on the information to the radio officers. From the Marconi Wireless Room, Jack Phillips and Harold Bride began frantically sending out signals to as many ships as they could. Three letters, "CQD" indicated the international distress call. "CQ" indicated it was a call to all ships while "D" signaled distress. The two men also sent out the new "SOS" distress call, and joked it would probably be their last chance to use it.

```
12.15am
CQD CQD CQD CQD CQD CQD
Titanic to all ships

12.34am
WHAT IS THE MATTER WITH YOU?
Frankfurt to Titanic

WE HAVE STRUCK AN ICEBERG AND SINKING. PLEASE TELL
CAPTAIN TO COME.
Titanic to Frankfurt

OK. WILL TELL THE BRIDGE RIGHT AWAY.
Frankfurt to Titanic
_____

1.10am
SINKING HEAD DOWN.
COME AS SOON AS POSSIBLE.
Titanic to Olympic

CAPTAIN SAYS—GET YOUR BOATS READY. WHAT IS YOUR
POSITION?
Titanic to Olympic
```

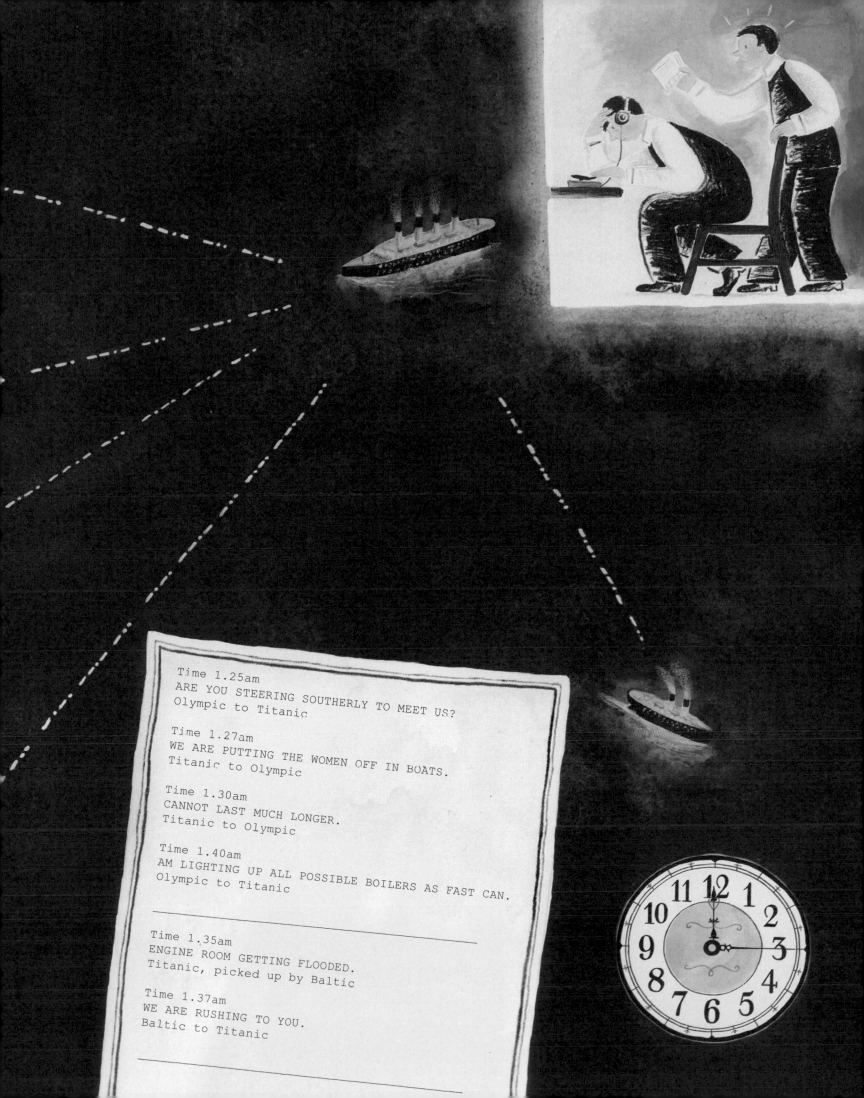

Time 1.25am
ARE YOU STEERING SOUTHERLY TO MEET US?
Olympic to Titanic

Time 1.27am
WE ARE PUTTING THE WOMEN OFF IN BOATS.
Titanic to Olympic

Time 1.30am
CANNOT LAST MUCH LONGER.
Titanic to Olympic

Time 1.40am
AM LIGHTING UP ALL POSSIBLE BOILERS AS FAST CAN.
Olympic to Titanic

Time 1.35am
ENGINE ROOM GETTING FLOODED.
Titanic, picked up by Baltic

Time 1.37am
WE ARE RUSHING TO YOU.
Baltic to Titanic

It was now forty minutes since the Titanic had hit the iceberg and many of its first class passengers had gathered in the lounge wearing their lifebelts.

Many struggled to believe the ship, which had been called "unsinkable", could truly be in danger.

Some passengers moved out onto the deck. The musicians followed and continue to entertain the crowds.

THE CARPATHIA RECEIVES AN "SOS"

Back on board the Carpathia, it was just after midnight. Cottam was preparing to finish his shift. He had been waiting up to hear a response to a message he had sent earlier in the day. After deciding he had hung on long enough, he contacted Titanic about wireless messages for her at Cape Cod.

"GM OM (GOOD MORNING OLD MAN). DO YOU KNOW THERE ARE MESSAGES FOR YOU AT CAPE COD?"

Carpathia to Titanic

12.25am
COME AT ONCE… WE HAVE STRUCK A 'BERG. IT'S A CQD, OM.

Titanic to Carpathia

Stunned and now sharply awake, Cottam tapped out a reply:

```
SHALL I TELL MY
CAPTAIN? DO YOU
REQUIRE ASSISTANCE?

Carpathia to Titanic
```

An answer quickly came:

```
YES. COME QUICK!

Titanic to Carpathia
```

Cottam ripped off his headphones, grabbed the sheet of paper bearing the message and ran to the officer on duty, First Officer Dean, and explained what had happened. Without hesitation, both men rushed to Captain Rostron's cabin.

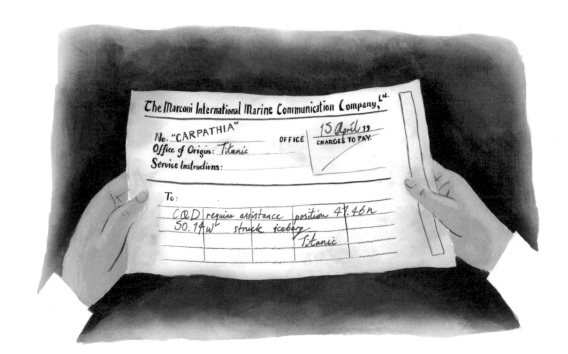

Cottam and Dean charged down the corridor and went hurtling into the captain's cabin without knocking. Before Captain Rostron could even respond, Dean uttered words he would never forget.

CAPTAIN!

WE'VE JUST RECEIVED AN URGENT DISTRESS MESSAGE FROM TITANIC!

SHE HAS STRUCK AN ICEBERG AND REQUIRES IMMEDIATE ASSISTANCE. HER POSITION IS 41.46 NORTH 50.14 WEST.

Are you absolutely sure?

Yes Sir.

Captain Rostron's mind was clear as he thought. He ordered Dean to return to the bridge and turn the ship around.

They were 58 nautical miles from the Titanic's reported location. At her customary top speed of 14 knots, it would take the Carpathia at least four agonizing hours to reach the sinking ship. They had to go faster.

ACTION STATIONS

Captain Rostron roused his crew into action. All hands were needed for the race to the Titanic and the rescue of its survivors. But as the Carpathia prepared to bravely forge a path through an ice-strewn sea, the Captain was only too aware of the dangers ahead.

ABOVE DECK

All hands turned to the rescue plan. They readied life boats in case they were needed for survivors. Ladders were placed at gangways to assist those climbing aboard. Canvas bags were set out to scoop up children.

The Purser, Assistant Purser, and Chief Steward prepared to receive survivors and note down their names so they could be sent to waiting relatives by wireless.

Second Officer Bisset had exceptional eyesight and was stationed on the starboard bridge wing. There he kept watch for any lights, flares, or ice. Additional lookouts were stationed in the crow's nest, on the port bridge wing and on the ship's bow.

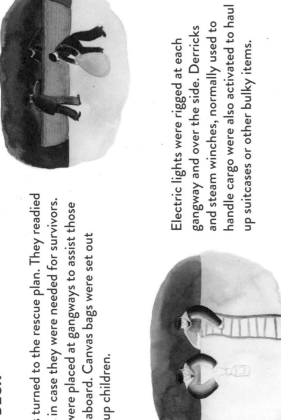

Electric lights were rigged at each gangway and over the side. Derricks and steam winches, normally used to handle cargo were also activated to haul up suitcases or other bulky items.

Bridge

Captain and Officer's quarters

Galley | Store Room | 3rd Class Cabins | Engineers Cabins | 2nd Class Cabins | 3rd class dining room converted to makeshift hospital ward

Hold | Engine Room | Boilers | Refrigerated Hold | Coal Hold | Refrigerated Hold | Hold | Hold

BELOW DECK

Preparations were made for the arrival of survivors. The Carpathia's dining rooms were converted into makeshift hospital wards each overseen by a doctor to welcome those in medical need. Blankets and hot drinks were prepared by a team led by Chief Steward Evan Hughes.

The captain instructed the Chief Engineer to wring every ounce of steam from the boilers to propel the ship forward. No energy was wasted. Even the ship's heating was turned off.

Captain Rostron implored his crew to carry out these tasks in complete silence. He didn't want to disturb the sleeping passengers.

Oil supplies were readied for pouring down the toilets. This technique would be used to calm the sea near the boat during the rescue, if required.

TITANIC'S LIFEBOATS

Meanwhile, the Titanic was taking on water fast. Lifeboat seven was the first to be lowered into the water on the Titanic's starboard side. There were only 27 people in it, but there was space for 65. Many passengers were terrified and reluctant to leave a ship they still believed would never sink. With only 20 lifeboats on board, there was only room for around half of the Titanic's passengers and crew.

Boxhall fired the first of up to a dozen rockets, hoping to catch the attention of any nearby ships.

CANADA

QUEBEC

MONTREAL

NEWFOUNDLAND

40° NEW YORK BOSTON

HALIFAX

GREAT BANKS OF
NEWFOUNDLAND

SABLE ISLAND

35°

X
X

30°

60° 50°

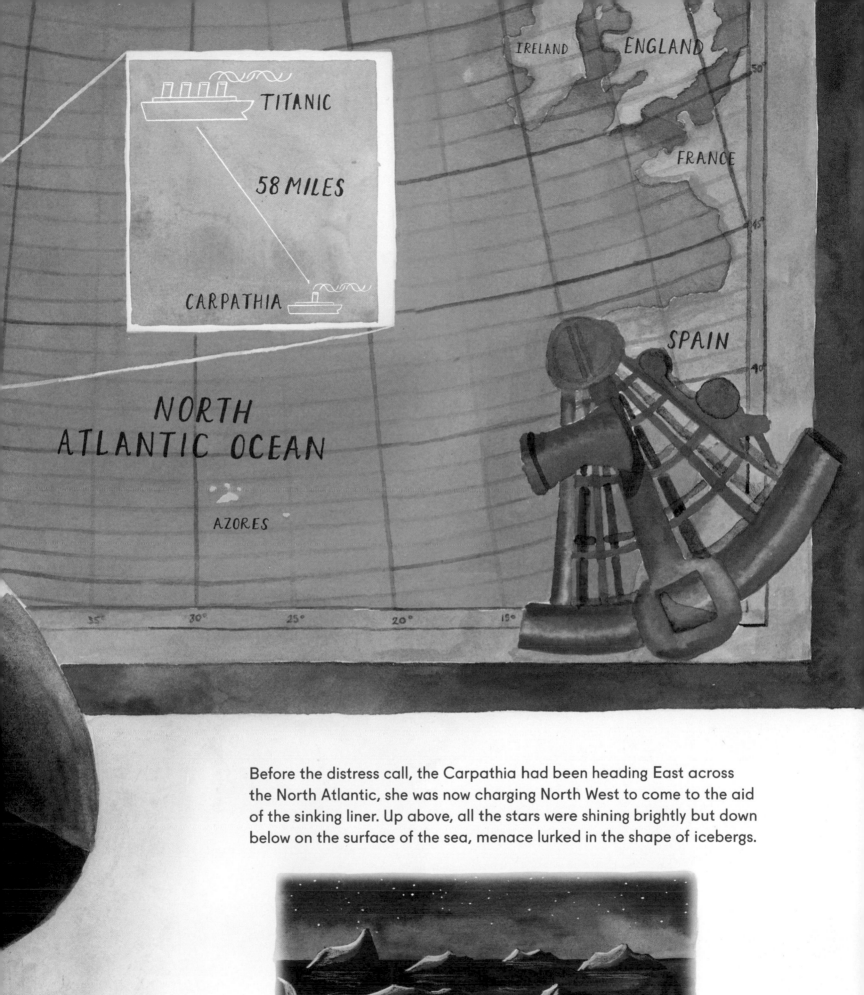

TITANIC

58 MILES

CARPATHIA

IRELAND ENGLAND

FRANCE

SPAIN

NORTH
ATLANTIC OCEAN

AZORES

35° 30° 25° 20° 15°

Before the distress call, the Carpathia had been heading East across the North Atlantic, she was now charging North West to come to the aid of the sinking liner. Up above, all the stars were shining brightly but down below on the surface of the sea, menace lurked in the shape of icebergs.

PANIC SETS IN ON THE TITANIC

Many of the Titanic's lifeboats had been lowered and panic was now rising. The Titanic's decks were filled with passengers searching for available lifeboats. The mighty ship pitched noticeably forward.

Lifeboat 13 was lowered, shortly followed by lifeboat 15. 15 almost landed on 13 which had drifted directly below it.

As the Titanic's lifeboats had room for only about half those on board, Captain Smith ordered that women and children were to be saved first.

Within the next half hour, Captain Smith relieved all crew of their duties. Valiantly, Phillips and Bride ignored the Captain's orders and continued to send wireless messages until the power ran out.

Captain Rostron and his crew held their breath as the Carpathia sped through the darkness, the light of hundreds of stars above reflecting off the eerily calm, inky waters. The Captain and Chief Engineer Johnston estimated the ship was now steaming onwards at around 17 knots, 20 percent faster than its normal top speed.

Although Captain Rostron turned all crew to the rescue cause, he worried about the risks to own his passengers. It was a dangerous mission. While he resolved to do all he could to help, he knew time was running out for the Titanic.

At 1.45am, the Titanic's wireless officer Phillips desperately implored Harold Cottam;

"COME QUICKLY AS POSSIBLE, OM. ENGINE ROOM FILLING UP TO THE BOILERS."

Although the Carpathia's crew had performed their duties as quietly as possible, some passengers were woken by the sound of activity on the decks. A small group, including the Ogden family ventured out on to the promenade deck and watch as the action unfolded.

A LIGHT IN THE DARKNESS

One of the ship's doctors, Dr. Frank McGee informed Captain Rostron that each dining room was prepped and ready to receive survivors. As they spoke, a green flare lit up the dark horizon on the Carpathia's port bow. "Titanic must be still afloat!" The captain explained. With a renewed sense of hope, Captain Rostron ordered his officers to fire rockets at 15 minute intervals to let the mighty ship know the Carpathia was on her way.

NAVIGATING THE ICE FIELD

Almost immediately after the sighting of the green flare, Second Officer Bisset spotted the ominous glint of starlight on a large mass on the Carpathia's port side. An iceberg loomed ahead. The Carpathia veered right to avoid it and cut its speed. Soon the ship was zig-zagging past berg after berg. The captain's quick reactions were crucial to keeping the ship afloat and saving the Titanic's survivors.

In addition to the rockets, the captain ordered his crew to begin firing Cunard company roman candles. When fired up into the sky, they looked like twinkling blue stars.

The Carpathia reached the Titanic's last reported
location at 4am. Captain Rostron stopped the
engines. He felt proud that his crew and his ship
had done everything he had asked of them.
They had worked tirelessly through the night,
spurred on by the thought of those in peril.

Captain Rostron also felt an increasing sense of hopelessness.
Despite their best efforts, the mighty ship was nowhere to be seen.
The last communication they had received from Phillips and Bride
was over two hours ago. They were too late. Under that moonless
sky sprinkled with stars, Captain Rostron and his crew felt very alone.

Suddenly, they saw a pale green glow not far ahead and low in the water!

SALVATION AND SORROW

The Captain and his crew sprang to action and approached the Titanic's Lifeboat 2, only narrowly avoiding collision with a berg as they did so. Bisset and two seamen climbed down rope ladders and jumped on board to help the survivors up onto the Carpathia.

As the first survivors came aboard, Captain Rostron learned that the Titanic had sunk completely at 2.20am. There was no time to lament, they must do all they could for the Titanic's survivors.

The sun was beginning to rise, revealing the rest of the Titanic's lifeboats bobbing nearby. The sunrise also revealed horrifying lumps of ice stretching as far as the eye could see.

They continued to pick their way carefully through the bergs, gradually picking up all of the Titanic's survivors from 18 lifeboats. A number of passengers were able to climb up rope ladders draped down the side of the Carpathia, while others were hoisted up on slings or chairs. Children were placed into canvas sacks and winched aboard. In all 706 passengers and crew survived the sinking.

Incredibly, 25 men kept alive by climbing on top of the Titanic's upturned Collapsible Boat B, among them was Harold Bride. They stayed there until daybreak, when they transferred to one of the lifeboats.

By 8.30am, all survivors has been rescued from the water.

MAKING SENSE OF TRAGEDY

Monday, April 15

Captain Rostron and his crew were struck by the immense quietness of the traumatized survivors as they came aboard the Carpathia.

The crew helped survivors out of their lifebelts. Stewards ushered them to the makeshift hospital wards and gave out blankets and hot drinks.

Soon after the survivors boarded the Carpathia, officers compiled a list of their names, a task which took most of the day.

The Carpathia's passengers did all they could for the survivors, giving them dry clothes to keep them warm. Many passengers, such as Colin and Emma Campbell Cooper, even made room for survivors in their cabins. Most importantly, everyone did their best to console the survivors and encouraged those overcome with grief to eat and drink a little.

Later in the day, a memorial service was held for those who had perished.

Captain Rostron decided the Carpathia must return to New York and bring the survivors to their intended destination. Their three-and-a-half day journey began with a detour around a large ice field.

WRITING HOME
Tuesday, April 16

After Harold Bride had been helped off the hull of the Titanic's Collapsible Boat B, the young radio officer was sent straight to the Carpathia's sick bay. One foot was badly sprained, the other frostbitten.

Meanwhile, the Carpathia's own radio officer, Harold Cottam had been working furiously to communicate news to the White Star Line and Cunard offices, particularly in sending out names of the Titanic's survivors. He hadn't slept in over two and a half days.

Overcome by extreme tiredness, Cottam was soon assisted by Bride who had to be carried to the wireless room because of his injuries.

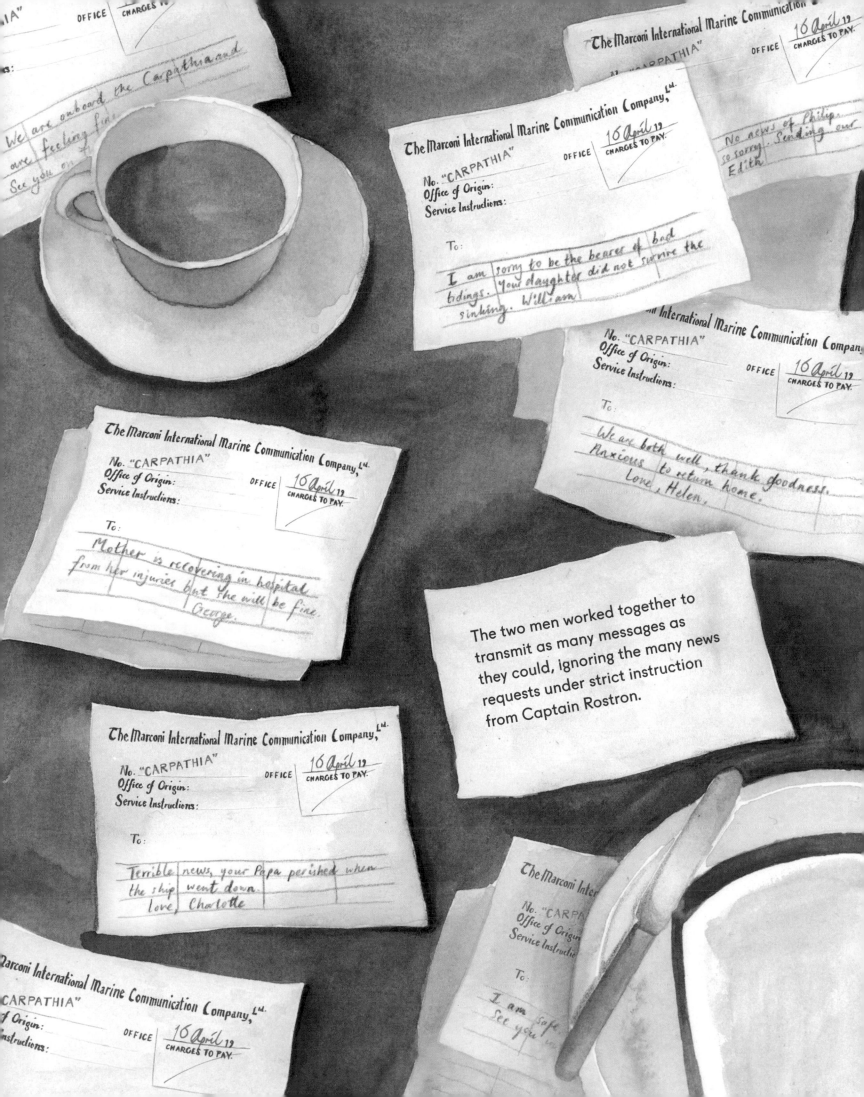

The two men worked together to transmit as many messages as they could, ignoring the many news requests under strict instruction from Captain Rostron.

HOMEWARD BOUND
Wednesday, April 17

The Carpathia's route back to New York was slowed by dense sea fog that engulfed the ship, while the threat of ice loomed everywhere.

During the return trip to New York, some of the Titanic's survivors, including Denver heiress and suffragette Molly Brown, decided to organize a Survivors Committee. They organized to collect funds to distribute among the Carpathia's crew and also to pay for medals to mark their heroic rescue effort.

Bernice Palmer, an 18-year-old passenger on the Carpathia, had watched the activity unfold on deck in astonishment. With her new Box Brownie Kodak camera in hand, she had documented all she saw. Bernice had even taken a picture of the iceberg which many thought had sunk the Titanic.

LAND AHOY!

Late on Thursday afternoon, the Carpathia reached the Ambrose Lightship, a floating lighthouse for guiding ships into the New York bay. It was surrounded by boats of news reporters eager to interview Titanic's survivors. Captain Rostron and his crew realized just how much the Titanic's story had captured the world's imagination. Huge placards were hoisted, indicating the newspaper the journalists worked for. The captain was determined no one would board his ship and disturb his passengers.

The Carpathia made its way up the Hudson, flanked by tug boats, yachts, and ferry boats. By 9pm, 30,000 people awaited the humble ship's arrival at Cunard's Pier 54. While the Carpathia's passengers and crew hung back, Titanic's survivors disembarked first. Reporters jostled into position and camera bulbs flashed wildly in the driving rain.

Exhausted, Captain Rostron and his crew heaved sighs of relief. They had done all they could and now, their task was complete.

RECOGNIZING THE HEROES

Captain Rostron and his crew received heroes' welcomes in New York. They were presented with medals from Molly Brown, of the Titanic Survivors Committee. Captain Rostron also received a commemorative silver cup.

Among numerous other accolades, Captain Rostron went on to receive a Congressional Gold Medal, a civil award created especially for him by the US Congress, and was knighted by King George V in 1926. He rose to the rank of Commodore within the Cunard Line.

A subsequent parliamentary report into the disaster recorded its great admiration for Captain Rostron's conduct.

"HE DID THE VERY BEST THAT COULD BE DONE."

GLOSSARY

BINNACLE—A case for housing a ship's compass located close to the steering position.

BRIDGE—Room where a captain or senior officer commands a ship.

BOSUN'S CHAIR—A seat suspended on a rope.

BOW—Front section of a boat or ship.

CAPE COD—A sandy peninsula extending into the Atlantic from Massachusetts, USA.

COLLAPSIBLE BOATS—Lifeboats built out of wood and canvas which can be folded up.

DERRICK—A crane for lifting cargo.

GANGWAY—Narrow passageway used by boarding or disembarking passengers.

GALLEY—The name traditionally given to a ship's kitchen.

GREENWICH MEAN TIME (GMT)—Time displayed at the Royal Observatory, Greenwich, a location on the Prime Meridian.

HULL—The watertight outer covering or shell of a ship.

KEEL—Beam running longways under a ship.

KNOTS—Unit of speed equal to one nautical mile per hour.

LATITUDE—A measurement of distance north or south of the equator.

LONGITUDE—A measurement of distance east or west of the Prime Meridian.

LUMBER—Wood already processed and cut into planks. Known as timber in the UK.

MAIDEN VOYAGE—A ship's first journey after the handover from its builders.

MASTER-AT-ARMS—Officer responsible for enforcing order and discipline on a ship.

MORSE CODE—An international system of dots, dashes and spaces which represent numbers and letters of the alphabet.

NAUTICAL—Concerning ships and sailing.

NAUTICAL MILE—Unit of distance equal to 1.852 km or 1.151 miles.

PORT—Left hand side of the ship as you look forward.

RMS—Ships contracted to transport letters and parcels for the UK's Royal Mail.

ROMAN CANDLES—Fireworks which throw out bright colored stars.

STARBOARD—The right hand side of the ship as you look forward.

STEERAGE—Lower deck accommodation for passengers paying the cheapest fares.

STERN—Rear section of a ship or boat.

TELEGRAM—A short message sent by means of electrical current or radio waves.

TRANSATLANTIC—A term used to describe travel across the Atlantic Ocean.

VICTUALLING—Title given to crew who look after cooking, stewarding and stores.

WINCH—A device for winding in or letting out a rope or cable.

SOURCES

Bäbler, Günter, *Guide to the Crew of the Titanic: The Structure of Working Aboard the Legendary Liner,* The History Press, 2017

Behe, George, *Voices from the Carpathia: Rescuing RMS Titanic,* The History Press, 2015

Butler, Daniel Allen, *The Other Side of the Night: The Carpathia, the Californian, and the Night the Titanic was Lost,* Casemate, 2014

Clements, Eric L., *Captain of the Carpathia: The seafaring life of Titanic hero Sir Arthur Henry Rostron,* Conway, 2017

Ludowyke, Jay, *Carpathia: The extraordinary story of the ship that rescued the survivors of the Titanic.* Hachette Australia, 2018

McCaughan, Michael, *Titanic: Icon of an Age,* Blackstaff Press, 2012

Rostron, Arthur, *Home from the Sea: The Autobiography of Captain Rostron of the Carpathia, the Man who rescued the Titanic Survivors,* Spitfire Publishers, 2018

FURTHER READING

Fullman, Joe, *The Story of the Titanic for Children,* Welbeck Publishing, 2018

Malam, John, *Titanic and Other Lost Ships* (Lost and Found), QED, 2012

Noon, Steve, *Story of The Titanic,* Dorling Kindersley, 2012

To the memory of Captain Sir Arthur Rostron
and the crew and passengers of the Carpathia.

With particular thanks to
Mum, Dad and David.

—F. D.

Brimming with creative inspiration, how-to projects, and useful
information to enrich your everyday life, Quarto Knows is a favourite destination
for those pursuing their interests and passions. Visit our site and dig deeper with our
books into your area of interest:
Quarto Creates, Quarto Cooks, Quarto Homes, Quarto Lives,
Quarto Drives, Quarto Explores, Quarto Gifts, or Quarto Kids.

First published in 2021 by Wide Eyed Editions, an imprint of The Quarto Group.
100 Cummings Center, Suite 265D Beverly, MA 01915, USA.
T +1 978-282-9590 F +1 978-283-2742 www.QuartoKnows.com

ISBN 978-0-7112-6278-2

The illustrations were created in watercolor and ink
Set in Noyh a Bistro, Fugue and Bodoni

Commissioned and edited by Lucy Brownridge
Designed by Karissa Santos
Production by Dawn Cameron
Published by Georgia Amson-Bradshaw

Manufactured in Guangdong, China TT052021
9 8 7 6 5 4 3 2 1

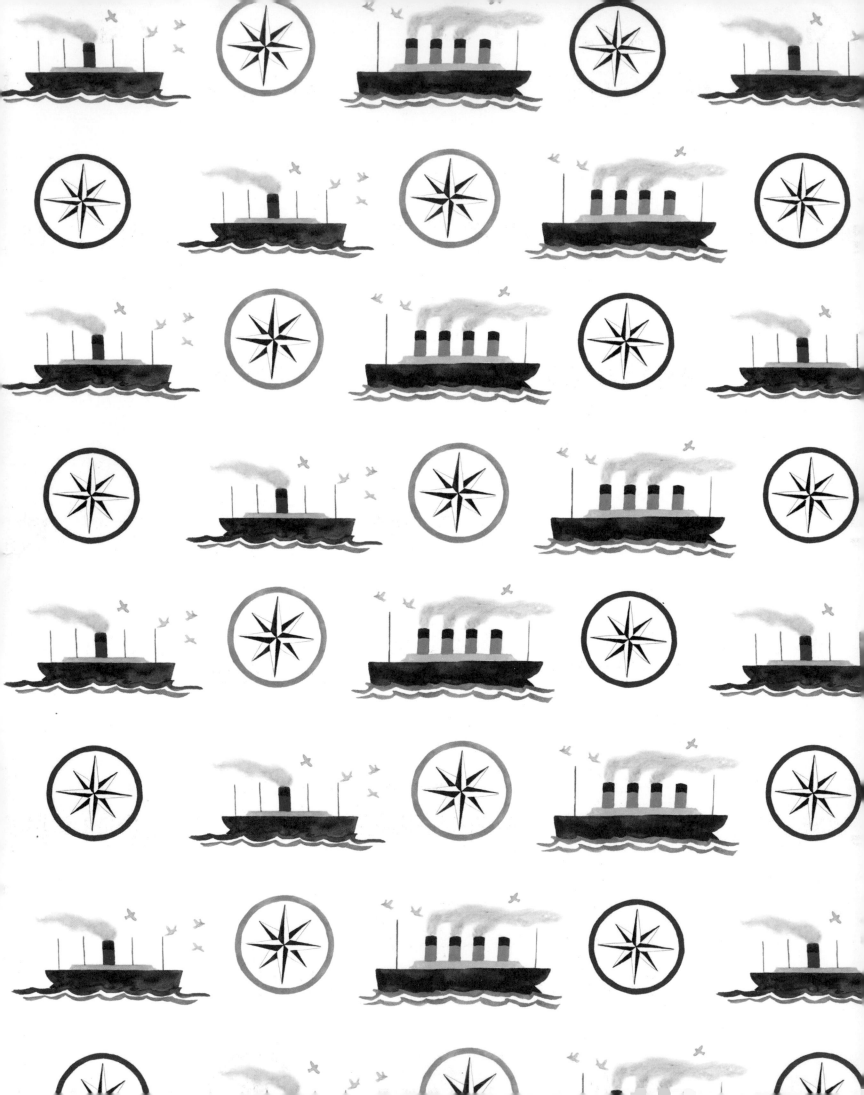